KT-568-079

The First Christmas

by Robbie Trent

pictures by Marc Simont

Julia MacRae Books

LONDON SYDNEY AUCKLAND JOHANNESBURG

Text copyright © 1948 by Robbie Trent
Illustrations copyright © 1948, 1990 by Marc Simont
First published in the USA 1948 by Harper & Row
First published in Great Britain 1991 by Julia MacRae
an imprint of Random Century
20 Vauxhall Bridge Road, London SW1V 2SA

Random Century Australia (Pty) Ltd
20 Alfred Street, Milsons Point, Sydney, NSW 2061

Random Century New Zealand Ltd
PO Box 40-086, Glenfield, Auckland 10, New Zealand

Random Century South Africa (Pty) Ltd
PO Box 337, Bergvlei, 2012, South Africa

Printed in Hong Kong

British Library Cataloguing in Publication Data
Trent, Robbie
    The first christmas.
    I. Title II. Simont, Marc
    813.54
ISBN 1-85681-021-6

The First Christmas

This is Mary.

This is the donkey
that Mary rode
to Bethlehem.

This is Joseph
who led the donkey
that Mary rode.

This is the town
of Bethlehem
where Mary and Joseph
were going.

This is the inn
where Mary and Joseph
could find no room.

This is the stable
where Mary and Joseph
rested in Bethlehem.

These are the shepherds
out in the fields
near Bethlehem.

These are the dogs
that were helping
the shepherds to keep
the sheep safe.

This is the moon
that the shepherds saw
in the night-time sky.

This is the angel bringing glad news, "Little Jesus is born in Bethlehem."

This is the road
where the shepherds
went running to find
the baby in Bethlehem.

This is the manger
filled with hay
that the shepherds saw
in the stable.

And this is the baby
the shepherds found
that First Christmas night
in the manger.

"Away in the manger,
No crib for a bed,
The little Lord Jesus
Laid down His sweet head;
The stars in the sky
Looked down where He lay,
The little Lord Jesus
Asleep on the hay."

Old Hymn